Stock Market For Beginners

The Ultimate Guide To Make Money With Stocks. Become A Profitable Trader With Proven Strategies And Create Your Passive Income

MATTHEW R. HILL AND HENRY KRATTER

1

Copyright 2021 - All rights reserved.

The content contained within this book may not be reproduced, duplicated, or transmitted without direct written permission from the author or the publisher.

Under no circumstances will any blame or legal responsibility be held against the publisher, or author, for any damages, reparation, or monetary loss due to the information contained within this book. Either directly or indirectly.

Legal Notice:

This book is copyright protected. This book is only for personal use. You cannot amend, distribute, sell, use, quote or paraphrase any part, or the content within this book, without the consent of the author or publisher.

Disclaimer Notice:

Please note the information contained within this document is for educational and entertainment purposes only. All effort has been executed to present accurate, up to date, and reliable, complete information. No warranties of any kind are declared or implied. Readers acknowledge that the author is not engaging in the rendering of legal, financial, medical, or professional advice. The content within this book has been derived from various sources. Please consult a licensed professional before attempting any techniques outlined in this book.

By reading this document, the reader agrees that under no circumstances is the author responsible for any losses, direct or indirect, which are incurred as a result of the use of the information contained within this document, including, but not limited to, — errors, omissions, or inaccuracies.

Table of Contents

Introduction 8

Chapter 1: Bull & Bear Markets 10

Chapter 2: Stock trading Mindset 14

    Get Yourself in the Right Mindset 15

    Have a Great Base of Knowledge? 16

    Imagine Winning 17

    Imagine Yourself Losing 17

    Always Practice 17

    Observe the Habits of Successful Trades 17

    Remain disciplined 18

    Be patient 18

    Understand the difference between historical volatility and implied volatility 18

Chapter 3: Trading VS Investing 22

    Am I a trader? 22

    I only have short term business goals 22

    I have more liabilities than assets 22

    I am not growth conscious 23

    I don't care about my knowledge level about the business 23

    I am not visionary about my business 24

    I have little or no value for my customers 24

    I don't invest in people 25

    I don't evaluate my business 25

    Key factor 25

Chapter 4: Diversification Tips and Guidelines 29

    Pros and Cons 30

Chapter 5: Make Sure you have the Right Tools to Trade Profitably 34

    Low Cost Trading Platform 35

    Fast Trading Platform 35

    Fast Updating Charts 35

    Solid Accountant 36

Chapter 6: Investing in Mutual Funds 38

How mutual funds work? 39

Fees and costs associated with mutual funds 41

Avoiding hidden costs and letting them eat your gains 42

How the fund charges fees may add up to extra expenses as well. 42

Passively Managed Funds..43

How to invest in mutual funds 43

Stocks vs. ETF vs. Mutual Funds – Which is Right for You? 43

Chapter 7: Exchange Traded Funds 46

The Advantages and Disadvantages 50

How to utilize ETFs and Where to Invest..50

Super Diversification with ETFs..52

ETFs versus Picking Stocks..53

Chapter 8: Stock Trading Strategies 56

Fundamental Analysis..56

The Process of Fundamental Analysis...57

Terms Associated with Fundamental Analysis.............................58

Technical analysis..59

Examples of technical analysis 60

Averaging down 61

Growth investing 62

Value investing...63

Stock split 63

Stock mastery...64

Develop your own 65

Chapter 9: When Is the Best Moment to Buy and Sell Stocks?...........68

When to Buy and Sell Stock 68

When a Stock Goes on Sale 68

When It Hits Your Buy Price 68

When It Is Undervalued...68

When You Have Done Your Homework...69

When to Patiently Hold the Stock...69

The Best Day of the Week to Buy Stock...69

Best Day of the Week to Sell Stock 70

The Best Day of the Month to Invest 70

Chapter 10: Money management...72

Chapter 11: Investor Psychology 77

Psychological Traps That Work against Investors 78

Anchoring Trap 78

Confirmation Trap 78

Relativity Trap..78

Superiority Trap..79

Develop a Clear, Concise and Workable Investment Strategy........................79

The Importance of Having an Investment Strategy......................................80

It Helps Minimize the Risk of Losses 80

It Helps Provide Clarity on Your Long-Term Goals.............................81

Opens You Up to the Possibility of New Opportunities For Your Business 81

It Helps in the Efficient Allocation of Time and Resources 81

Criteria for Developing a Good Investment Strategy....................................81

Make Sure Your Strategy Fits with the Overall Direction of the Investments
....81

Be Sure Your Strategy Matches the Resources You Have at the Moment.. 82

You Need to Monitor the Business rather than the Price of Stock 84

Analyze the Numbers 84

Performance of Management 84

Chapter 13: Bonds and Government securities..86

Bonds in detail 86

Bond Pricing..89

How to Invest 89

Conclusion 91

7

Introduction

A swing trader doesn't need to sit at his computer watching the stock markets all day long, although you certainly can if that's an option for you and you like doing it. Swing traders can also start small and grow their business over time.

While substantial profits are attainable, it's not a get-rich-quick scheme and although it can be done on a part-time basis, we want you to start thinking of swing trading as a business from this point forward. The goal is to earn profits, and you can use those profits as ordinary income if you like or reinvest them to build your retirement account or some combination of the two. That is entirely up to you. But keep in mind one thing: very few people are going to make a millions in their first year and slide into retirement.

Swing trading is about taking a short-term position in the market whereby you identify recurring patterns in a stock price line, and then use that to ride the wave and make a profit. It can be described best as the middle ground between the highly hectic and stressful world of day trading and the much more academic and studious approach of position trading. In swing trading, though, you are working on positions that last more than a day but, in most likelihood, less than a week, as you should focus on only one leg of a swing. That means you have the luxury of time to research and hone your strategy but not too much time to over think things.

Swing Trading is by no means easy, but if you follow the advice in this book you will firmly have put the odds on your side, you will be confident in trading with the correct strategy in the market as well as in balancing your risk and reward dilemma - and you can't really ask for more than that.

Swing trading can be a great way to earn a big profit in a short amount of time to the stock market. Start learning more about swing trading with this guidebook that's designed to provide you with concise information.

9

Chapter 1: Bull & Bear Markets

The stock markets often trend in one direction of the other. When the economy is faring well, interest rates are low and companies are thriving, then the stock markets will follow suit and thrive. When the markets thrive, it means the prices are generally going up. This upward trend is referred to as a bullish run and the market is said to be a bull market.

On the other hand, when the economy slows down, interest rates are high, and the outlook is poor, then the markets are likely to follow suit and stock prices will fall. This leads to a bearish run and the market is said to a bearish market. In the US, the markets have been on a bullish run since 2009. As such, most new traders have probably only experienced a bullish market but never experienced a bearish one.

According to historic figures, bull market runs are often followed by bear markets. This is the norm as bear markets are also always followed by bull markets. The Bull Run that started in 2009 began just after a recession which happened in 2007/2008. Bull markets imply investor confidence in the markets while a bear market signifies a lack of confidence in the markets. The best part is that bull markets last for far much longer periods of time compared to bear markets. So, there's a possibility to grow your portfolio over time as the stocks are likely to overcome bear sessions.

Sometimes a stock market can experience a crash. This is a situation where stock prices drop drastically. This tends to affect the performance of different stocks but especially investor portfolios. Though, another piece of good news is that a correction will take place and the markets will be restored. However, stock market crashes are quite rare. When they happen, they do point to a potential bear market.

So, as a potential trader, always think about researching before buying any stocks. Research is the way and will draw the line between success and failure. If you are unsure about the research, then you'll be better off seeking professional advice.

Your broker is one such expert. He can provide you with the advice that you need to invest wisely. Although, this advice does come at a price and it will cost you. Plenty of experts believe it is much better and safer to pay for advice rather than take risks and possibly lose money. Therefore, seek advice where you can and use it appropriately.

13

Chapter 2: Stock trading Mindset

Mindset dictates how we handle situations and is made up of assumptions and judgments. Our mindset is affected by our conscious, subconscious, and unconscious minds. The basic organization of these levels of our psyche fit together in way in which mindset affects each. We make judgments according to our mindset. For example, you may be happy about one thing while the person next to you is sad about the same thing. Our mindset is made up of our brain's communication with the outside world, memories, and experiences. It is the latter two that shape our beliefs and habits, forming our behavior. Although, this is not a dissertation on cognitive psychology so we will stick to the topic of how mindset can make a positive difference in your approach to investing in the stock market.

There are important skills an investor should possess. The following are entrepreneurial skills the benefit an investor.

Take responsibility for your decisions, whether good or bad. Own your mistakes and celebrate your successes.

Get out of your comfort zone. We are creatures of habit. We do what's easy. To break out of your habits and strive for making a difference, get out of your comfort zone.

Be prepared for continuous learning. Investing isn't a static skill. It's a path of continuous learning where thirst for knowledge equals success. The smartest entrepreneurs are constantly evolving and changing their approach based on learnings and market feedback.

Understand that time is treated differently when investing. Often you'll be making decisions based on uncertainty. Short-and long-term goals require different approaches. What you do (or don't do) today will have an impact down the road. Imagine if you bought stock in Apple 30 years ago!

It's about the numbers. Numbers are the indicators of your investment's success or failure. Pay attention to and learn to understand what the numbers are telling you. This means understanding a stock's prospectus and not just looking at its returns in the last 12 months.

Trust your instincts. If it doesn't feel right, don't do it! But do not confuse trepidation with that feeling of excitement and newness. With some experience you will begin to tell the difference.

Emotional decisions are often regrettable and the same is true for making emotional investment decisions.

There are several methods you might employ in order to maintain your composure. Popular methods include diversification, staggering buy and sell decisions, choose dividend paying stocks, and limiting investments in volatile commodities, such as oil. Basically, focus on metrics, be objective and willing to change your investment strategy depending on your goals and market performance.

Get Yourself in the Right Mindset

It is advised that as a trader, ensure that you always participate in self-motivation exercises and pep talks daily. You can greatly benefit from simply reminding yourself things like stock prices are not personal. The most effective way of getting a positive state of mind for stock trading is by giving yourself the gift of time. Suppose you are this type of person who wakes up at 8:00 am and then brushes through study before the trading day begins, then you're likely to approach to trading with a state of mind that is flustered and rushed. This makes it hard to do trade as an expert. Develop a culture of waking up earlier so that you can always have enough time to acclimate to the day. If possible, you should always meditate before starting your research. This will enable you to approach trade from a mentality that is more relaxed. Before starting your daily trade, take some time and get your head in the right place because this can positively impact on your trading activities. Having a calm mind may not be able to remove your emotional reactions when doing a trade but can be of great help in reducing the potential damage that comes from making quick decisions.

Have a Great Base of Knowledge?

One of the best ways to cultivate the best trading mindset is to increase your knowledge about the trade. When you have a strong base of knowledge on how trading works, you can come up with better decisions. Gaining technical prowess about the ways with which trading works will give you better ways to find solutions and make rational decisions thus you will be able to react in a very calm manner.

Think about this way: You were made to oversee a project by your boss. You have been doing this project for the last three weeks and now it's complete. So, on the night to the presentation day, you decide to polish through the project and prepare for the presentation which will be done early in the morning. But with bad luck, your operating system crushed and shows you a blue screen. Because it's late and the presentation is early tomorrow, you have to come up with a solution. You have little knowledge of IT, but you must find a solution. You will have to do some detailed research before approaching this problem. From your research, the first solution suggests that you can do OS repair and restore your personal computer to its normal state. This first solution warns you that if you aren't careful with following the instructions, you might as well end up formatting the whole machine. The second research solution tells you that you can simply do a reinstallation on the PC and you can get all your data in the say windows. old folder. Suppose you had good knowledge in IT, you would simply repair it in a more relaxed and calm way.

In this case, by researching the issue, you were able to know the risks involved and how to come about solving the problem. This is like trading. Trading without proper knowledge can make us come up with decisions based on fear or greed. To develop the best mindset for trade, ensure that always educate yourself as this is the only way you will minimize the risks involved in trading. Having a strong foundation of knowledge will enable you as a trader to make a rational and informed decision.

Imagine Winning

We have seen Olympic athletes visualizing themselves are winners of a game or race. Coaches usually tell their trainers to see themselves as winners. Well, players may not get to win but this visualization helps them no to hurt their performance. Why don't you do the same as a trader? Visualizing yourself as a winner can be very motivating and can play an significant role when you're trying to figure out the real steps you need to take to achieve your goals as a trader. Physical inspiration can also play a great role. You can have a physical list of your goals or even have a visualization board in your room showing the photos of the things you would like to achieve once you make a substantial earning. By simply imagining the winning scenario, you can feel so inspired and have the desire to achieve more.

Imagine Yourself Losing

As you expect the best, also prepare for the worst. While it's essential to visualize a big win, it's also important to take a few moments and consider how you might feel if you lose. Imagining the worst-case scenario will help in keeping you away from making foolish decisions or mistakes. You will take proactive steps to avoid such negative outcomes.

Always Practice

You won't be skilled at something if you don't practice. Trading requires that you acquire and develop skills and strategies. Successful traders work hard and practice a lot. Time is usually the biggest teacher. Practice enables you to gain mental strength in trade. You should always practice every tip, every little skill that you gain.

Observe the Habits of Successful Trades

When it comes to trading, don't copy the trade strategies of another trader because this may work against you. Trading has many variables thus you'll never copy the exact method that you use to trade and expect to win. It advised that you only observe the positive characteristics seen in successful traders and then cultivate these aspects in you.

Remain disciplined

Many new traders find themselves going after specific stocks or types of stocks simply because they have a gut feeling. Unfortunately, very few people can effectively trust their gut when it comes to trading stocks which means this scattershot policy will not only make it more difficult for you make a profit overall, but it can teach you bad habits along the way as well. In this case, a better choice is to instead work on building your trading discipline by following the rules outlined below with every single trade you make.

Be patient

While it's likely for an investor to pick the right investment at the right time and become extremely wealthy practically overnight, this is without a doubt the exception not the rule. If you hope to make some serious money using the stock market, it's necessary that you settle in for the long haul. There are no trading plans that are 100 percent accurate and anything more than 60 percent is considered accurate enough to trade with on a regular basis. What this means is that it is unrealistic to expect a flawless trading history and that you'll lose out on trades, even those that seemed like a sure thing, every single day.

Understand the difference between historical volatility and implied volatility

Implied volatility should be one of the main gauges you use to determine if a given stock is priced appropriately. As a rule, the higher the amount of implied volatility, the more bearish the market is going to be, and the more expensive various stocks will be. Although, it should not be the only thing that you consider which means that historical volatility is just as crucial when it comes to choosing profitable cheap options correctly. You can study the historical volatility of a given stock by plotting it out beforehand in order to determine the difference between the general volatility and the current amount of volatility.

21

Chapter 3: Trading VS Investing

Understanding the difference is key. This is because it is often the difference between working from hand to mouth and attaining financial freedom. Do you want to have financial freedom? I can hear you say "of course, I do!" Then, you need to understand the key differences between investing and trading. Get set for some simple but powerful tips that will change your life forever!

Am I a trader?

I will deal with this by helping you know who a trader is. Once you know who a trader is, you can easily recognize an investor. You are a trader if you are found doing the following things discussed below:

I only have short term business goals

Traders are only into business with the aim of getting quick cash. They are only trying to make ends meet. Hence, you're a trader and not an investor if you have the habit of just getting the short-term profit, a business has to offer and never plan about the long-term sustainability of the business. This will make you go into a business deal asking questions like, "What is in it for me?", rather than "What is the long-term benefit I can get from this business?" When you have short-term goals as a business person, you will have the tendency to invest in businesses that will crash quickly.

I have more liabilities than assets

You are also a trader when you have the tendency to acquire more liabilities than assets. Liabilities are those things you buy simply for the sake of enjoying them. They only take from you. I mean, you'll need more money to maintain them while they offer nothing in return apart from the satisfaction of using them. You're probably thinking about some people in your life right now that perfectly fits that description. Well, bad news; I am not talking about people, I am talking about things. "Oh, my car, my house, my dog…" There you go again; I am not talking about animals either. "But my car and houses aren't animals!" Well, I am not saying that too.

I am not growth conscious

Traders have this attribute in common: they are never growth conscious. They only care about harvests. Everything just needs to be quick! Quick cash, quick fixes, shortcuts, easy routes, and similar attributes only considered admirable by fellow traders. Traders only think about getting it right now! Patience is never in their dictionary. They see people who are willing to wait for a business to blossom before they start reaping the dividends as fools. In the long run, by the time investors are reaping the dividends of their patients, traders can only bite their fingers in regret as they reap the dividends of their haste.

I don't care about my knowledge level about the business

Traders are terrible learners. All they care about is the profit. They don't care whether they have a good knowledge of the business or not. All they need is someone who can convince them that they will make some cool cash from a business, and they are good to go. As a result of this poor attitude to thorough research, traders are often caught in the web of trending businesses. Assuming a lot of people are investing in a business and they claim they are making a profit; they will invest in the business too.

Investors don't follow that trial and error approach. They take their time to study the business and ask the right questions from the right people. This helps them to make quality decisions about the businesses they invest in. Traders are often in a hurry to invest in anything in vogue. If you're just a trader, you won't be able to give sound answers when people ask you questions about the business you have chosen to invest in.

Investors weigh the pros and cons of the business objectively before they invest in it. They don't just invest because their friends and families are investing in it. They study the long-term sustainability of the business too. They ask questions such as "is the business seasonal?", "is it dependable?", among others. They can predict to a very good extent, the pattern of the business. There is no excuse to be ignorant in this age about anything. There are lots of information surrounding us, especially via the Internet. Investors take advantage of this in order to make quality choices regarding their business decisions.

I am not visionary about my business

Investors have mastered the act of being able to see a forest in a seed. All a trader sees in the seed is the opportunity to cook to eat or roast it and eat it. "If it cannot be eaten at the moment, it is not worthwhile." That is the mantra of a trader.

Traders aren't visionary about their business. They can only see them now because their decisions do not emanate from a thoroughly planned thinking. Hence, you're a trader and not an investor when you have the tendency to only see what is happening in the moment. Investors know the phase the business is at every point in time because they have planned it beforehand. They understand the likely challenges they might face at a stage of the business and they have plans to solve the problem.

I have little or no value for my customers

Investors understand that they need the trust and loyalty of their customer in order to be able to maintain the long-term sustainability of the business. Hence, they only operate by making customer-friendly policies when making decisions concerning their business. They always think about what their customers want. They are interested in the feedback they get from their customers. They use these feedbacks to improve in every area of the business in order to please their customers. This will, in the long run, make the customers feel that the business cares about them. The result of this is that the company has more customers which translates into more money in the long run.

Hence, a trader is only interested in making money but an investor is very concerned about pleasing the customers while making money. Both the investor and trader are trying to get to the same destination: making a profit. Though, they go through different routes to get to their destination. The trader will get to the destination but will crash-land. The business will arrive at the destination with a lot of scars.

I don't invest in people

You are a trader when you are only concerned about things and not people. In other words, investors aren't just fond of investing in businesses, they are also fond of investing in people. I am not trying to paint a picture of a lofty idea here. What I mean is that, because an investor is concerned about the long-term growth and development of their business, they will be very interested in the growth and development of their staffs. What this means is that an investor is ready to upgrade the skills of people who work with them in order to bring about an increase in productivity.

I don't evaluate my business

Traders only wait for things to go wrong before they think about how they can improve the business. Provided they are making a profit, traders don't have the luxury of time to evaluate the business. They only have one way to evaluate whether the company is doing fine or not - more money.

Investors are always on the lookout for rooms for improvement. They do this by getting feedback from their customers. They also do this by consulting experts who give them tips to improve their business through branding and other means. They are never satisfied with whatever level of success they have attained.

Key factor

If you have been paying good attention, you will notice that the key factor that distinguishes a trader from an investor is long-term planning. While an investor is always thinking long-term, a trader is always thinking short-term. Most of the other differences that have been identified between a trader and an investor hinges on this factor. The reason a trader does not set out time to evaluate their business is that they only have short-term goals. The reason a trader does not have value for their customers also emanates from this same premise.

Investment in people, being visionary about the business, being knowledgeable about the business, being growth conscious, and acquiring more assets rather than liabilities are all linked to this attribute. Hence, without controversy, we can safely conclude that the key difference that distinguishes a trader from an investor is the fact that while a trader has short-term goals, an investor has long-term goals.

28

Chapter 4: Diversification Tips and Guidelines

Diversification is a chief strategy for investing. As a financial term, it means simply distributing your investments in various industries for stocks, combining different financial assets, and creating a mix of these assets that will enable you to meet your investment goals. But in the world of investing, diversification refers to a very specific strategy of investment—the careful selection of assets that would react in different ways to an event.

So far, we have identified the events that create market volatility and make investing in the stock market a risky endeavor. A portfolio combines shares with ETFs, REITs, trust funds, bonds, and other assets, but if not done properly, it can combine assets that react the same way or in a similar manner to events in the economy.

With diversification, you put together stocks that fit together like a cogwheel so that every drop in the price of a particular asset is counterbalanced by a rise in the value of another. So, the price of oil stocks rises, and airlines will charge higher prices because of it hence reducing their business. Their stocks will drop.

The inverse is true as well. Having a stock from each sector in your stock portfolio means that your portfolio is balanced regardless of what happens in either industry. If the oil and airlines industries combination does not appeal to you, then you can trade out oil with railway companies. When anything happens to reduce traveler confidence in the airline industry, railroads experience a surge in travelers and vice versa.

Another fantastic combination of assets that can help you keep your portfolio balanced out is that of stocks and bonds in general terms. Stocks normally drop in price when interest rates climb, a time when the price of bonds climbs. Most investment gurus define diversification as simply ensuring that you don't bet on the same horse for long. This hypothetical horse represents the geographical location, economic sector, and investment type.

Pros and Cons

The benefits of diversification have been addressed at length above. The main reason why we diversify, however, is that it allows you to secure your investments against market volatility and keep your investment stable.

Another advantage of diversification is that it allows us to cover our bases. By thinking about the risk quotient of assets before choosing to invest in them, we can identify potential hurdles before they become too problematic. For one thing, diversification forces us to think about our risk tolerance, which is the foundation for a good portfolio.

One of the biggest drawbacks to diversification comes from a very curious aspect of the diversification process—choosing your assets. With so many assets to choose from, you might get stumped, unable to choose between different assets.

Another disadvantage of diversification is that it demands that you select stocks from different, unrelated industries. Choosing between good assets in the same market sector could result in you leaving the best one of them all and you have to then watch as it rises in price without taking advantage. The opportunity cost of choosing one stock over another could be very demoralizing.

Another con to excessive diversification is that the balancing out of assets in your portfolio whereby a rise in one asset is met by a corresponding drop in other leads to average returns. The cost of trying too hard to ensure that your portfolio will bring you no losses is the fact that you can never make much money. The former hinders the latter.

Another drawback to diversification is that you are more likely to incur massive costs while trying to balance it out by constantly buying and selling.

Yet, it is definitely worthwhile diversifying. A diversified portfolio gives you confidence because it assures you that your investment is secure. Just make sure you don't overly diversify or micromanage the risks associated with the assets on your portfolio.

Diversification goes along with portfolio management. The more closely you monitor your portfolio, the better you can diversify. If you think the passive style of portfolio management does not pay enough attention to the assets in your portfolio, a midway point between active and passive portfolio management can allow you to hit the sweet spot between over-diversifying and not doing it thoroughly enough.

Traders must have a certain mindset when it comes to investing. Investing in stock takes a lot of self-discipline. There is a certain psychology that traders must become familiar with to have success in their investments. There is a whole investing mindset that must be utilized to drive results.

Investors must detach themselves from their emotions when investing in stock; otherwise, they risk trading out of fear and greed. Investors must also not become too attached to any stock. Although there is an art to investing, it's always advised that investors utilize logic to drive their actions.

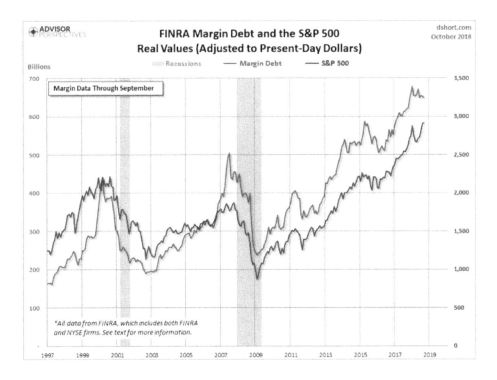

33

Chapter 5: Make Sure you have the Right Tools to Trade Profitably

If you're thinking of either buying into a mutual fund or trading individual stocks directly, you need to have the right tools. This is imperative. A lot of newbie investors think that one online brokerage is essentially the same all others. This is assuming too much, really.

You might be leaving a lot of money on the table by going with one online broker over another. You must know what to look for. If you're just going to go by brand or by word of mouth, this might work against you. You might end up paying too much, seriously. You can pay too much in two ways.

First, you can pay too much in terms of just flat out higher fees. Different online brokers have different fees per trade. Some charge by volume, others charge by value, others charge a flat fee. Even among those that charge based off flat fee, their fees can differ.

The second way you pay is in terms of execution. You might be thinking, well if I order this stock to be bought and I bought it, where's the harm? Well, if you're using a platform that is fairly slow, you might not be getting the best price. It may be so slow, that you buy well after a pullback.

Meaning, if you're looking to buy into a stock, ideally you should buy in when the stock suffers a pullback or goes down in value. Now, the problem is if the trading platform is so slow, the pullback may have happened and now the stock is quickly recovering. And instead of for example buying a $30 stock at $25 pullback level, your platform gets you in at $27. You just lost $2. It might not seem like a big of a deal, but if you have a margin account and you're trading tens of thousands of shares, that can translate to a lot of money lost.

Do you see how this works? You need make sure that you pay attention to the following factors when looking for the right tools to trade profitably. It doesn't really matter whether you're going to do multiple trades every day or you're basically just investing the stock market and adopting a position trading strategy where you just check in from time to time. This is also applicable if you are a value investor and you're just basically locking in now and then checking in once a year or twice a year.

Low Cost Trading Platform

The first thing that you need to look at is whether the platform is low cost. Compare the platform to other similar platforms. Look at their service package. What's the limit? How many shares can you buy and at what price before the commission or fee goes up? Make sure you compare apples to apples because some trading platforms use different fee schedules to try to trick you, but it turns out that on an aggregate basis, you may be paying more so do yourself a big favor.

Fast Trading Platform

You must make sure your trades are executed as quickly as possible. Insist on a very fast platform because you may be out of a tremendous amount of money if you're investing in stock that is a high momentum or extremely volatile stock. It can be going up and down frequently with almost every trade and you want to lock in at the right price. This is much harder to pull off if you're using a trading platform that is slow.

Fast Updating Charts

If you're a daily trader or a swing trader, you need charts. You need as much data in your charts so you can make the right call. You also need to make sure that you use charts that are updated frequently enough.

Go with real time updated charts as far as you can. This enables you to make quick calls to seize pricing opportunities. For example, if a stock fell through the sport price and it looks like it's experiencing a nice pullback, you want to be able to see that pattern play out in real time on your chart so you can make moves and capitalize on that change. This is very hard to do if your charts are unavailable or they update very slowly.

Solid Accountant

Taxes are a big issue if you're going to be trading stocks. US tax code treats stock trading income as regular income. Unless you're value investing and you just buy and sell stocks with more than one year intervals, you would have to pay regular income taxes on your trading income.

So, it is imperative to insist on solid accounting from your trading platform. The good news is by law, almost all trading platforms that offer their service in the United States have a solid accounting infrastructure. At the very least, your gains are being tracked, so you can report them to the IRS.

Make sure you use the right tools. If you want to increase the chances of you trading profitably, you really cannot afford to use the wrong tools because at best, you'll be leaving a lot of money on the table and at worst, you'll be losing out.

Chapter 6: Investing in Mutual Funds

A mutual fund is a professionally managed group fund that invests in a diversity of assets. It seeks to balance risk and reward carefully, and it's not a get-rich-quick type scheme. The more careful an investor you are and the more you would prefer having a professional manage your money, the more likely you are to seek out a mutual fund. There are downsides, though. Having a fund be actively managed means it costs money to manage the fund – so you can pay fees that can significantly eat into your investments over time. Second, there isn't solid evidence that a professionally managed fund does better than a diverse portfolio that isn't managed by an expert.

In a mutual fund, a pool of money is created to buy stocks and other types of investments. The fund is managed by a professional money manager who does the thinking for you. The money manager is a trained professional who knows how to create a balanced portfolio that pits the right amount of risk against the right amount of caution to develop an investment vehicle that should be profitable over time. Of course, money managers aren't all the same, and some funds will perform better than others.

A key strategy used in the creation of mutual funds is diversification. That is, rather than buying stock from one, two, or three companies; a mutual fund manager will buy stocks from a wide variety of companies

Mutual funds can be active, that is the manager of the fund actively picks stocks to include in the fund and decides when to buy or sell individual stocks that make up the fund. It's unclear that actively managed funds provide a clear benefit to investors. Even for a trained professional, trying to handpick winners and losers in the stock market isn't all that easy. You need to pay fees for an active fund manager as well.

Mutual funds provide ease of investment while being relatively safe investments. They also often require only small monthly commitments, so it's not necessary to invest large sums of money all at once.

One particular risk of mutual funds is known as "dilution." In short, this means doing too much diversification in search of safety. At some point, diversifying across too many stocks might result in a situation with minimal returns or stagnation.

How mutual funds work?

Let's start with the word mutual. The definition of mutual is "experience or done by two or more parties...held by two or more parties for the benefit of all parties involved". From this definition, we see the first aspect of mutual funds, which is a pool of money gathered from multiple investors into a single fund for the mutual benefit of all.

Fund simply means a sum of money saved for a particular purpose. In the case of a mutual fund, the fund is saved for the purpose of investing in stocks, bonds, and other assets.

A mutual fund has some investment objective in mind. For example, one fund might focus on aggressive growth (high earnings) while another focuses on stability and regular income (think – more bonds). The professional money manager that deals with the fund will select the stocks, bonds, and other investments to put into the fund to meet its specific goals. Investments are spread across a wide variety of companies, incorporating multiple business types and sectors. This is done to spread your risk and hence reduce it. Not all stocks are going to move in the same direction, and not all industries or business sectors will either. By investing widely across businesses, industries, and sectors, we average out the risk so that the entire fund isn't put in danger by the collapse of one or a few companies or a downturn in a sector.

A mutual fund is divided into *units*. There is a cash value assigned to a unit based on the value of the underlying investment, so units are issued to each investor in proportion to the amount of money they put into the mutual fund. The value of each unit is called the *Net Asset Value* or NAV. This is the current market value of a single unit in the funds holding. So, if the total value of the fund were $100,000, and there were 100 units in the fund, the NAV would be $1,000. Investors buy units in the fund priced at the NAV. So, the number of units an investor can buy depends on both the NAV and the amount invested. So, if NAV is $20 and an investor puts in $20,000, then they own 1,000 units.

Of course, it's always changing as the holdings in the portfolio rise and fall with each trading day. An important thing to remember about mutual funds as opposed to trading individual stocks or ETFs is that they only trade once a day, after closing.

It's useful to know the NAV per unit for the mutual fund. This is given by the market value of the underlying securities minus the total recurring expenses, and then you divide this number by the total number of units in the fund. Note that the number of units in the fund may not be fixed – so we need to know the number of units on a specific date.

There are two very significant factors associated with mutual funds – strategy and fees. Fees are so indispensable that we discuss them separately in the next two sections.

Basically, a mutual fund will take one of four different strategies related to growth. A general rule is the more aggressive growth, the higher the risk.

Aggressive growth: This is a high risk/high reward type of fund. The types of companies that are used for a fund with an aggressive growth goal include newer companies in high tech, startups, or companies in emerging markets: more risk but more potential for bigger earnings.

Growth and income: A more conservative approach that focuses on large-cap U.S. companies ($10 billion or more). Moderate to low risk, considered stable investments.

Growth: This focuses on large U.S. based companies that are growing, but companies that are smaller than those in the growth and income type fund. These are medium to large sized companies (or mid-cap to large cap) valued between $2 billion and $10 billion. They will tend to have higher returns than those in a growth and income fund but are less stable. They are subject to more influence by the economy at large and will move up or down with the economy.

International: This type of fund focuses on large companies outside the United States. It may be stable, as it focuses on well-known international companies.

Although our discussion has focused on stocks, you need to realize that a mutual fund can also invest in bonds, cash, and money market funds. So, another way to look at it is the more growth-oriented the fund, the fewer bonds and cash investments that will be in the fund. A fund can be entirely weighted toward bonds and cash investments, set up for low risk and income.

If you decide to invest in mutual funds, you'll need to do some upfront investigation. Don't just jump in feet first with the first mutual fund that you find. Look at comparable options offered by different investment companies. You'll want to seek out a fund that closely aligns with your goals, although many advisors suggest investing in multiple funds, splitting your money evenly between the four general types outlined above. If you're getting closer to retirement and are more interested in protecting your principal, then you should opt for investing in low risk, income-oriented funds. No matter what you do, check the long-term history of the fund and compare it to important benchmarks like the S & P 500. Do you want a fund that doesn't perform as well as the S&P 500? What would be the point of that? You could just invest in the S&P 500. It's a good idea to take the performance period to be at least ten years. You don't want to get suckered into buying a fund that hasn't done all that well over the long-term but had a good run the last year or two.

Fees and costs associated with mutual funds

Since a mutual fund is *actively managed,* there are going to be costs associated with it. It costs money to have someone else set up your investments, buy and sell shares on your behalf each day, provide customer support, and produce shiny reports for you to look at. These are the operating costs of the mutual fund, and they aren't going to eat them – they are going to make you pay the operating costs. So, an essential part of investing in mutual funds is seeking out a mutual fund that has reasonable fees.

Avoiding hidden costs and letting them eat your gains

The type of expenses we listed in the last section fall into the category called ongoing fees, sometimes known as annual operating expenses. These are the basic costs of the fund manager running their business. These fees are bundled together into a fee called the expense ratio. The industry average is 0.64% and can range from 0.5% to 1.0%. Some funds have expense ratios as high as 2.0-2.5%. If you find a fund with a large expense ratio, you need to figure out why it's high and if it has certain benefits that offset the higher cost. If not, it's best to turn to another fund because those expenses will eat into your earnings.

For example, suppose you invested $10,000. If the expense ratio was 0.68%, then your fee that you'd pay annually would be $68. On the other hand, if it was 2.5%, then the fee would be $250. That is a significant difference. Let's use a more realistic example, comparing two funds over the course of 20 years. We will set the initial investment at $100,000. Then, we'll add an additional $5,000 each year, and assume the fund has an average growth rate of 6%. Now, we'll have a fund A, which has an expense ratio of 0.64%, and fund B, which has an expense ratio of 2.5%. At the end of the 20-year period, the expenses/fees that you would have to pay to fund B would be $115,514 higher than the expenses/fees you'd pay toward fund A – a lot of missing money that you could have used for your retirement or pay a significant expense.

You can try an online calculator for yourself here:

https://www.nerdwallet.com/blog/investing/typical-mutual-fund-expense-ratios/

How the fund charges fees may add up to extra expenses as well.

There are other fees to be aware of:

● Transaction fees – These are one-time fees that are incurred when the fund manager makes a change in your investments.

● Commission fee: Charged when buying shares.

● Redemption fee: Charged when selling shares.

● Exchange fee: Charged when taking shares in one mutual fund and putting them into another.

● Account service fees: charged when you invest a smaller amount of money than some cutoff set by the fund.

The bottom line: small differences in fees can add up to huge amounts of money over a 20-or 30-year period, significantly corroding investments. Choose wisely.

Passively Managed Funds

A passively managed fund will have far lower fees, with an expense ratio on the order of 0.2%. In a passively managed fund, your money is invested in some index fund like the S&P 500.

How to invest in mutual funds

The best way to invest in a mutual fund is to contact one of the larger companies that sells them. You can visit any investment company but consider Fidelity or Vanguard and contact them about investing. If you own your investment account, you can also buy mutual fund shares on your own.

Stocks vs. ETF vs. Mutual Funds – Which is Right for You?

If you want to play an active, and direct role in your investments, stocks are exactly where you want to be. If you're interested in the freedom that comes with stock trading, including being your own money manager, but want the built-in diversification that comes with mutual funds, then you might be an ETF type person. If you're more safety-oriented and would prefer having a professional managing your investment portfolio, then you might be in the market for a mutual fund.

45

Chapter 7: Exchange Traded Funds

Exchange traded funds are my favorite kind of investment. You'll see why in a second. Mutual funds are diversified, and it is easy to invest in mutual funds using dollar cost averaging. But they cost money, and you have little control, which you've handed over to a money manager. Also, mutual funds only trade once a day after the market closes.

Buying stocks gives you more direct control. Rather than having a money manager you have to pay to carry out his services, including making copies at the office, paying for phones and other incidentals you probably don't like paying for, with stocks you're the one doing the trading. This has some risks, but for those who want control over their investing, it has appeal. Also, you may like the flexibility of being able to buy and sell any time the markets are open. Although, due to the buying power of a large group of individuals and a money manager who is working on the markets full-time, it's hard to get the kind of diversification and other benefits that you're going to get with mutual funds.

What if you could wave a magic wand and combine the best of mutual funds with the best of stocks? Well, it turns out that you can. The result is the exchange-traded fund. When you boil everything down to basics, and this is an unmanaged mutual fund that trades like a stock.

An ETF gives you automatic diversification – its biggest advantage. Even if you don't exclusively trade in ETFs, it's a good idea to have them as a significant portion of your portfolio.

Typically, an exchange-traded fund will track stock index. There is a wide array of exchange-traded funds; they also track bonds, real estate, cash, commodities, currencies, and baskets of assets. The price of ETFs changes throughout the day as they are traded on the major stock exchanges. So, buying or selling an ETF is just like buying or selling a share of Apple or General Motors.

Like with mutual funds, you may see a lot of discussion of asset classes on websites for investment firms that have created ETFs. There are five asset classes:

- Stocks

- Bonds

- Money market instruments (cash)

- Commodities

- Real estate

In contrast to mutual funds, in addition to being able to trade them in real time rather than waiting for an end of the day settlement, many ETFs have larger volumes than mutual funds. They also have lower fees, in some cases much lower. As a result, they are a very attractive option.

For the beginning investor, ETFs are highly recommended. It's a way to get in on your own and have some protection by utilizing the built-in diversity that ETFs have. You can buy ETFs using market orders through your own online brokerage if you know the ticker symbols of the funds you want to buy. They are a great way to do individualized dollar cost averaging. You can buy shares at regular intervals as part of your investment strategy.

The low-cost core is the first class of ETFs we will look at. These are divided into:

- U.S. Equities

- International Equities

- Fixed Income

If you click on U.S. equities, you will see that there are several funds that have different options for tracking major parts of the stock market. For example, they have three options available for tracking the S&P 500:

47

- Growth

- High-Dividend

- Value

If you look under the general category for U.S. equities (not the low-cost core), you will see that you can also simply track the S&P 500 using SPY. Our friends at State Street work like a mutual fund, in the sense that they've used a large sum of money to buy stocks in the 500 companies that make up the S&P 500. You can buy small shares of it. At the time of writing, the stock is priced at about $285 per share.

However, SPYG – the S&P 500 Growth fund – is only $37 a share (prices will vary, by the time you read this). The fund also tracks the S&P 500 index but gives you a low-cost way to get in the market. Although, this fund is designed to tap companies in the S&P 500 they are believed to have the most growth potential. According to the website, they base this on the revenue growth, price to earnings ratio, and momentum of the companies chosen for the index.

You can also use SPDR ETFs to invest in preferred stock or commodities. GLD allows you to buy gold shares. NANR is a natural resources fund that you can use to invest in energy, metals, mining, and agriculture. You can also invest in bonds, loans, U.S. government treasuries, and overseas investing like China or Japan.

SPDR is not the only company out there. A recent arrival on the scene is a company called Robin Hood. This company has a mobile app that is used to trade on your smartphone or tablet. One advantage of Robin Hood is that it's commission free. It also allows you to invest in options and even cryptocurrencies, as well as directly in stocks.

Vanguard, a very popular investment firm known for mutual funds, also offers several ETF options. Their S&P 500 indexed fund VOO is one of the most popular investment options.

Another one of the big players in the ETF world is iShares by BlackRock. They are offered in four asset classes:

- Equity (stocks)

- Fixed income (bonds)

- Real estate

- Commodity

You can also invest by region:

- United States

- Europe

- Asia/Pacific

- Global

Or by market:

- Developed

- Emerging

For example, iShares offers a fund which tracks the Russell 2000. According to the website, had you invested $10,000 when the fund was started in 2000, today you've had about $40,000. The fund invests in smaller publicly traded U.S. companies that have long-term growth potential. Like investing in an S&P 500 index, this fund will give you a chance to invest simultaneously in all companies that make up the index – in this case, the 2000 small-cap companies on the Russell 2000.

If you look at the expense ratios, you see where you can get big advantages over a mutual fund. Expense ratios on iShares go as low as 0.04, with most around 0.19-0.20.

Remember these funds trade like stocks – so you don't have to enroll at iShares to buy iShares funds. You just have to know what the tickers are, and you can sign up with any brokerage firm to buy the funds as part of your everyday trades.

Note that while we've often talked about the S&P 500, you can invest in exchange-traded funds that track all markets. For example, the PowerShares QQQ fund tracks the NASDAQ 100.

The Advantages and Disadvantages

Although it's hard to say that ETFs have disadvantages, if you would rather hand over control to a money manager, then an ETF isn't for you because trading and investing in exchange-traded funds requires your active and direct participation, and there is no expert who is going to pick the right funds for you.

Nonetheless, they are fairly low risk due to the instant and automatic diversification within these types of investments. So, if you follow some basic investment common sense, you're good to go. The flexibility is a major advantage, but you shouldn't abuse it. In other words, when you decide to invest in a fund unless there is some very serious compelling reason to get out – stay in that fund. ETFs represent an opportunity for solid, long-term investing.

How to utilize ETFs and Where to Invest

You invest in ETFs at your regular brokerage. You should use the websites of major funds to educate yourself about what funds are on offer and what the goals are of each fund. That way you can carefully select funds that meet your investment goals.

You can also compare funds offered by one company to another, as to examine performance. SPDR also offers a small-cap fund that tracks the 2000 smallest publicly traded companies in the United States. How do the two funds compare?

• The iShares fund is larger, with 282 million outstanding shares, compared to about 40 million for the SPDR SPSM fund.

- Both have a similar P/E ratio of about 16.

- The expense ratio of the SPDR SPSM fund is 0.05%. For the iShares fund, it is 0.19%.

- The price of a share of SPSM is about $30, at the time of writing the iShares fund is $154 per share.

- Year to date, the iShares fund is up 15.8%, the SPSM fund is up 17.3%.

You might ask why the funds track the same index but don't offer the same performance. The reason is that each company makes its own decisions on the weight given for investments. For example, we can look at the top ten holdings of each fund. For the iShares fund we have:

- ETSY

- TRADE DESK INC-CLASS A

- FIVE BELOW INC

- CREE INC

- HUBSPOT

- PLANET FITNESS INC. CLASS A

- CIENA CORP.

- PRIMERICA INC.

- ENTEGRIS INC.

- ARRAY BIOPHARMA INC.

For SPDR's SPSM fund the top ten holdings are:

- MR. COOPER GROUP INC.

- TRADE DESK INCORPORATED CLASS A

- PLANET FITNESS CLASS A

- VERSUM MATERIALS INC.

- CREE INC.

- MELLANOX TECHNOLOGIES LTD.

- ITT

- ARRAY BIOPHARMA INC.

- COUPA SOFTWARE INC.

- INSPERITY INC.

As you can see, while there is some overlap, the different funds have given different weights to different companies, hence the top ten lists turn out different. The difference isn't all that significant, but you may note that the SPDR fund has performed a little better on a YTD basis. Over the past five years, the five-year market price of the SPDR fund has grown 7.59%, in comparison to 4.46% for the iShares fund. So, the SPDR fund hasn't just done better recently, it is done better for the past five years. That coupled with its lower costs (both the share price and expense ratio) make it a more attractive option in our view. But we aren't here to advocate for one or the other, but rather to give you an idea of how you might do your own analysis with these types of funds.

The lower share price of the SPDR fund will make it more accessible for those who are starting out with a lower budget or who don't want to risk large amounts of capital.

Super Diversification with ETFs

As we stated at the beginning and illustrated by looking at a couple of funds, ETFs provide automatic diversification, the same kind you get with mutual funds but without the costs, constraints, and hassles. If you want to build a solid, diverse portfolio consider picking your favorite ETF company and buying into all of their funds over time, or a diverse subset of them. Since there are funds that invest in stocks, bonds, real estate, and commodities, it's pretty easy to build up a portfolio that meets your investment plans, whether you're playing it safe and looking for an income-based portfolio or looking for an aggressive growth or maybe some balance in between.

ETFs versus Picking Stocks

ETFs trade like stocks, but they are not investments in individual companies.

Where did ETFs come from?

The history of exchange-traded funds traces its roots back through mutual funds. The first mutual fund was developed in 1774 by a Dutch merchant. At that time, he used pooled investing to allow people to invest in a closed-end fund. A closed-end fund has a pooled amount of capital that it raises through an IPO, and it's managed by a professional money manager. In modern times, closed-end funds are publicly traded funds themselves. From 1774 until modern times, mutual funds were the only game in town when it came to index funds.

The first attempt to launch an exchange-traded fund came in the United States in the late 1980s when there was a fund indexed to the S&P 500. But a federal judge actually struck it down, saying the fund had to be traded in futures markets. This ruling kept the fund out of the reach of ordinary investors, but soon afterward the first true exchange-traded funds were brought to market.

In 1990, an exchange-traded fund was introduced on the Toronto stock exchange in Canada, which tracked 35 large Canadian companies. This was soon followed a few years later by the creation of the S&P 500 Trust, an ETF that was created by our friends the State Street Global Advisors SPDR. This fund caught fire and remains popular till this day, and as we've seen, State Street has massively expanded the funds they have available with investing possibilities in virtually every asset class and market segment, both here in the United States and globally.

At first, ETFs were primarily used by institutional investors. Although, their use quickly caught on, and financial advisors and individual investors became interested in using exchange-traded funds to invest. Between 2000 and 2010, the total amount invested in ETFs grew from $0.1 trillion to $1 trillion, and by 2017 that figure had grown to $3.4 trillion.

Chapter 8: Stock Trading Strategies

You cannot achieve a consistent flow of profits just by relying on luck. To significantly increase your chances of success, you should use effective strategies. Take note that just reading about these strategies isn't enough. Investing in stocks is like learning a new skill. You also need to practice it. Let us discuss some of the notable strategies that you should know:

Fundamental Analysis

Fundamental analysis is the process of determining the intrinsic worth of any security by examining certain factors. The factors considered could be economic, financial, or other socioeconomic factors. Those generally affect the value of a stock, bond or any other such security.

Fundamental analysts carry out in-depth research concerning the various economic and other factors that affect the price of stocks. The factors that affect a security's value are broadly categorized into macro and microeconomic factors. Under this broad classification, you would find things like earnings per share, profits, price to earnings, *etc.*

In the process of analysis, the analyst may make use of either the top-down or bottom-up methods. In certain instances, also, he could employ a combination of the two.

In using a top-down analysis method, the entire market is taken into account. This is mostly within the field of macroeconomic factors. Also, the specific sector may be considered, or alternatively, the industry is considered instead. The last to be considered in this system is usually the stocks themselves.

Though, in the bottom-up analysis, the specific stock is first considered. Then every other factor follows subsequently.

What fundamental analysis seeks to achieve is to accurately predict which securities are valuable and which aren't. Fundamental analysis attempts to give the individual a fuller picture and the possible movements of the security either upwards or down. With such information, the investor can either go long or short depending on how the company fared.

If there is anyone who has proven time and again the effectiveness of fundamental analysis, it is Warren Buffett.

There are specific factors that are considered in fundamental analysis. They are as follows:

- Earnings-per-share: This is simply the amount of the entire profits assigned to one stock.

- Projected earnings growth: Here, the anticipated growth rate of the company for one year is calculated.

- Price-to-Book Ratio: Here, the stock's book value is compared with its value in the market. The book value is the value assigned to an asset by the company. The price-to-book ratio of an asset is arrived at by dividing the stock's recent closing price by the previous quarter's book value per share.

- Dividend Payout Ratio: Here, what is compared is the dividend paid out to the shareholders is then compared with the total net income of the company.

The Process of Fundamental Analysis

The fundamental analysis makes use of actual data in the public domain to evaluate a stock's worth. It can be used to evalutate every form of security, not just stocks. For example, an investor can employ the tool of fundamental analysis in evaluating a bond. In doing so, they would be mindful of the general economic landscape at that time.

He would also seek information concerning the company issuing the bonds. Certain factors, such as a change in the credit ratings can impact his final summation concerning the bond.

For stocks, the process of fundamental analysis differs a little. Fundamental analysis makes use of revenues, earnings and sometimes, profit margins, to determine the growth potential of the company.

Here also, the investor looks at the financial statements of the evaluated company.

Terms Associated with Fundamental Analysis

Fundamentals

This refers to the quantitative information about a company which is used for its evaluation. Investors analyze the fundamentals of a company to determine whether the assets found are worth investing in. Business potentials, assets, liabilities, *etc.* are often regarded as the fundamentals of a company.

Quantitative and Qualitative Analysis

Quantitative analysis makes analysis the same way a machine works. The analysis makes use of exact numbers and figures without any room for subjectivity. Inputs that can be made of include debt ratios and profit margins.

In quantitative analysis, exact outcomes are also projected using the exact inputs used. Thus, for instance, the exact profitability of a stock or the estimated growth of a company can be projected using quantitative analysis. Currently, the programs to run the analysis have to be written by humans.

For qualitative analysis, the parameters used for the analysis aren't as clear cut as found in quantitative analysis. The concerns here are often unscientific and are usually within the realms of the social sciences.

Risk Analysis

Risk analysts are often hooked into finding out what could go wrong. This then measures the possibility of the event happening. At the end of these steps, the investor can then take appropriate precautions. Furthermore, an investor can check for several outcomes using such tools like scenario analysis and sensitivity tables.

Risk analysis can be quantitative or qualitative; and this has been explained above. The same method employed is also employed this time, with specific attention being given to risks.

Technical analysis

If you are the visual type of person, then you might find this strategy interesting. Technical analysis makes use of graphs and charts to study the price movements of a stock. The idea behind this strategy is that the different factors that can affect a stock have their final effect on its price. Therefore, just by analyzing the price movements of a stock, you also deal with all the factors that influence it. You might want to consider this as the simplified and visual version of fundamental analysis.

When you use this strategy, you should learn to read patterns. Okay, you might be wondering: "Do patterns really exist?" The answer is 'yes.' In fact, even a random generator creates patterns. Although, it should be noted that patterns come and go. What this means is, you cannot expect to see a pattern all the time. There will be times when no matter how hard you study a graph, there is simply no pattern to be seen. Again, you don't need to worry because this is normal. A common mistake is forcing yourself to see a pattern even when no pattern exists. Remember, always make your analysis with a clear and unbiased mind. It is better for you not to proceed with planning than forcing yourself to see something which isn't even there.

Just like fundamental analysis, technical analysis can be used together with another strategy. In fact, many expert traders use both fundamental and technical analysis at the same time. Indeed, the more information that you have, the more likely it is that you can come up with the right investment decision. Technical analysis is an excellent method for short-term investments, but it can also be used for long-term investments.

Examples of technical analysis

The technical analysis foresees that the price continues to bounce on the trend lines as in the figure above until it breaks a support as in the figure below to accelerate sharply. These are great times to enter the market.

Averaging down

This strategy will allow you to purchase stocks at a bargain. You can then sell them for profit. The best way to explain how this works is by using an example. Let us say, you want to buy the stocks of company X, and its current price is $10 per stock. You then make a buy order at the said rate. If its price increases, then you can easily sell it for profit. Now, if the price decreases, then according to this strategy, you should make another buy order. So, if the price drops, say, to $9, then you should make a buy order at $9. Now, if the price decreases again, then make another buy order at the lower price. This way you are buying stocks at a much lower price.

Okay, you might be wondering: "Are you not simply buying a losing stock?" Although it may look like it, this isn't actually the case. In fact, you are making a sound investment. Just imagine how much profit you could make once the price of the stock goes back to its original price (its price when you first applied the strategy) or higher. All the buy orders that you made will give you a nice return on your initial investment.

Now, it should be noted that this approach is considered highly aggressive, so be very careful every time you use it. The key here is to identify a stock that will most likely increase in price. Take as much time as you can to research the stock concerned, as your success will depend on whether its price will increase or at least recover shortly.

A good strategy to use together with averaging down is fundamental analysis or technical analysis. You cannot use averaging down alone on its own as it relates only to the amount that you invest and does not tell you where to make an investment. Of course, where you put your money in is a crucial factor when it comes to making profitable investments. This strategy will allow you to weather fluctuations in the market since you're holding on to profitable stock investments. Again, keep in mind that although this seems highly practical, it's still considered a highly aggressive approach.

Growth investing

This is where you invest in the stocks of a company because you believe that the company has a potential to grow. This is usually used for small and start-up companies since they have room for development. When you use this strategy, watch new businesses. Consider how they are positioned in the market. Can they match up with the competition? Do not just focus on the company. Keep in mind that the strengths and weaknesses of a business are relative to the strengths and weaknesses of its competitors. Hence, you should also keep an eye on competing businesses. This is a good way to gauge how a business is doing in the market. It isn't enough that a company has space to grow, but the business should take positive actions to grow even further. Last but not the least, you should also pay attention to market acceptance. After all, no matter how amazing a business is, it will not do any good if the market ignores it or simply does not accept what it offers. These are the significant things to consider when you use this strategy. The drawback of using this strategy is that since you will most likely be dealing with start-up companies, there may not be enough information that you could use to measure the profitability of these companies. This is a challenge that you must overcome with this strategy.

Value investing

This is like growth investing. But in this case, it is the value that you need to view. When you use this strategy, you should look for a company that offers its stocks at a price that is lower than their actual value. Okay, this is where the challenge is. It is you who will have to determine the value of their stocks of the company. You need to look for stocks that are underpriced in the market. The idea behind this strategy is that the value of the stocks will soon adjust and correct itself. When this happens, and if you find a company that is underpriced, then you'll soon gain a nice profit. Unlike growth investing, value investing does not just work on new companies. It can also apply to old companies or stocks. Still, this is a good strategy to use on new and start-up companies since they tend to have good value but have a low stock price. It's good to use this strategy together with fundamental analysis. Take as much time as you need to study the company. Of course, do not forget to compare its strengths and weaknesses with the strengths and weaknesses of its competitors. If you find a company that has good value but is underpriced, then that is an opportunity that you can take advantage of. When you use this approach, it is imperative that you should not be biased about anything. Always keep an open mind and do your best to understand the company before you make any real investment.

Stock split

In a 'stock split,' a stock is split, and so it gets divided. For example, if a stock or share costs $40. After a stock split, then you'll end up with two stocks at $20 each. Take note that it does not always have to be an equal split. The point is that the stock will be divided, and so its price should also be divided accordingly. This is usually done by companies when the price of its shares gets too high. So, they move for a stock split to lower the price. This is also because investors tend to shy away from stocks that are too pricey. Now, this is a good sign. It usually means that the business is doing good. Normally, after a stock split, the price of stocks continues to increase. When you use this strategy, you should pay attention to companies that just declared a stock split. This normally signifies that they're doing well.

Now, you should be careful. A common mistake is to fall for a reverse split. This is like a stock split, but it isn't good. In a reverse split, stocks are combined, which causes the price of stocks to increase. Since there is an increase in price, it might look as if it were a good investment, although that isn't really the case. Here is an example. Let us say that there are 10 stocks at $10 each. In case of a reverse split, then you'll end up with five stocks at $20 each. This is the opposite of a reverse split. In this case, the price of stocks increases not because the company is doing well, but it's because of a manipulative action made by the company. Hence, do not forget that a simple increase in the price of stocks isn't good enough of an indicator that the company is doing well.

Take note that, although a stock split is often a good indication that the company is doing well, you should still do your own research before you make an investment. A stock split alone isn't enough. You should take a closer look at the company and study it carefully. This way you can increase the chances of making a good investment.

Stock mastery

The more that you know and understand a stock, the more likely that you can predict its price movement. This is the idea behind this strategy. When you use this approach, you should choose a stock that you like which you think is profitable. Your job is to make sure that you read and analyze the said stock every day. After some time, you'll notice that since you know the said stock so well already, you can easily predict its behavior in the market, and this will allow you to take advantage of it and make a nice profit.

Read and find out as much as you can about your chosen stock. Now, it's also common that you might suddenly realize that the stock isn't a profitable investment as you study it. This is well and good because it will help you lower your losses. In this case, do not be discouraged. Simply move to another stock and start over. Do not consider your efforts as a waste. If you end up with a losing stock, then be thankful for the fact that you have saved money by not making any real investment.

Once you gain mastery over a stock, then you can start taking advantage of it. But, how do you know if you have mastered a stock? There is no strict rule regarding this matter. The important thing is that you can predict its price movements correctly most of the time. Once you attain mastery over a stock, then feel free to go for another stock. The more stocks that you get to perfect, the better chances you have of making a large profit. Do not rush the process of learning and researching information about a stock. Take note that you're aiming for mastery, and not just having mere knowledge of a stock.

Develop your own

As a professional investor, you can develop your own strategy. It can be as simple as making a few adjustments to the strategies that you already know, but you are also free to come up with an entirely new strategy of your own. The life of a full-time investor is mostly about developing a strategy. Keep in mind that the stock market is a continuously moving market. The strategy that you use should be up to date with the latest changes and developments. Therefore, as you work on your strategy, you should also keep a close eye on the stock market.

Developing your own strategy can take a long time. Be ready to go through some trial and error before you adopt a strategy and apply it using real money. This is a good time to make use of the demo account provided by your stockbroker so that you can test your strategy in a real market environment without risking any real money. If you don't want to make use of the demo account, then you can simply make small investments and see how they go.

Take note that strategies are highly sensitive. This means that even a minor change in your strategy can make a big difference. On that account, when it comes to developing your own strategy, be sure to test it more than once even if you only need to make a small adjustment.

67

Chapter 9: When Is the Best Moment to Buy and Sell Stocks?

When to Buy and Sell Stock

When a Stock Goes on Sale

In our daily lives, as consumers, we tend to look out for deals when we do our shopping. For instance, Charismas seasons offer the best deals where prices are usually very low on highly demanded products. This is the time you'll see large-screen televisions or even phones being sold at an extremely low price. However, for investors, this is somehow not the case. Investors are usually not thrilled when stocks go on sale. The stock market is characterized by the herd mentality thus most investors tend to avoid stocks when prices are low.

When It Hits Your Buy Price

The first thing that you need to do as an investor is to estimate the worth of stock. This means that you will know whether a stock is on sale and likely to rise to the value you estimate it to rise to. It's preferable that you avoid coming to a single stock-price target but rather, you should establish a range at which you would purchase a stock. The good starting point can be analyst reports and consensus price targets because these two will give you the average of all analyst opinions. These figures are usually published by most financial websites. As investors, without the price target range, you are likely to have trouble determining when to buy a stock.

When It Is Undervalued

For you to determine that a stock is being undervalued, you need to go through a lot of information to effectively establish a price target range. In most situations, estimating a company's prospects is the best way of determining the level of undervaluation or overvaluation. A discounted cash flow analysis is the key analysis technique that will help you determine the future projected cash flows and discounts of a company based on the company's present condition. By getting the sum of these values, you will theoretically get a price target. From a logical perspective, if the current stock price listed is below this value, then make a purchase because it is likely to be a good buy. Another valuation technique that you can use is the comparison of the price-to-earnings multiple of a company's stock to that of the company's competitors. You can also choose to use other metrics like price to cash flow and price to sales to help you determine if a given stock looks cheap or expensive compared to its key rivals.

When You Have Done Your Homework

Well, a good starting point begins with checking the advice of newsletters and analyst price targets. Although, exceptional investors are ready to do their homework on a stock. This can involve reading annual report reports of a company, going through a company's most recent news releases and doing a thorough online check to identify some of the recent presentations a company has done to investors or their recent industry trade shows. There are companies that will avail all this data through their website particularly under the investor relations page.

When to Patiently Hold the Stock

Assuming that you have carried out research on your homework and have been able to properly identified the price target of a given stock and that you have also estimated that this particular stock has been undervalued, just hold patiently because such a stock will not have a value rise anytime soon. It usually can take time for a stock to trade up to reach its true value. If you see analysts projecting that prices will rise over the next few months or even the next quarter, such analysis is simply guessing that the value of a stock will rise quickly. This is because it can take a few years for a stock to fully appreciate its target price range. It would, then, be better that you consider holding a stock for even 3 to 5 years; but this is only if you're confident that the value will grow.

The Best Day of the Week to Buy Stock

Mondays are the suggestions of many. There are investors who believe that there are some days that offer systematically better returns compared to other days. Although, there is very little evidence about this belief. All in all, there are investors who believe that that Monday, the first day of the workweek is usually the best. This is usually referred to as the Monday Effect. One common trend that has been observed in the stock market for decades is the tendency to have price drops on Mondays. Some people believe this may be attributed to bad financial news released over the weekend. Others believe that on Monday most investors have gloomy moods as a result of coming from a weekend. But generally, everybody seems to hate Mondays. Therefore, if you're planning to buy stocks, you'd rather do it on a Monday.

Best Day of the Week to Sell Stock

Given that Mondays are usually the best days for buying stocks, then by default, Friday is also the best day to sell a stock, particularly before prices get low on Monday. Suppose you an investor who is interested in short selling, since stocks tend to have higher prices on this day, Friday is your best day for taking a short position and then Monday would be the best day for you to cover your short.

The Best Day of the Month to Invest

There is no single day of the month that has been identified to be ideal for selling or buying. But there is a common trend in the stock market where it has been always observed that stocks rise at the turn of a month. I think this is because at the beginning of every month, there is usually periodic new money flows usually directed towards mutual funds. Furthermore, it's a common trend for fund managers to usually try to identify exceptional quarters and buy stocks from these quarters all in the attempts to make their balance sheets look pretty. Generally, stock prices have always been seen to fall towards the middle of the month. This means that as a trader, you are likely to benefit from timing stock buys when approaching mid-month (between 10th - 15th) and the best day to sell stocks is usually within the first five days as we turn to a new month.

71

Chapter 10: Money management

The amount of money one makes in trading is solely dependent on the time they spend on the market. This is a major motivating factor since there are times when some stocks are selling lower and gaining more. Thus, when a beginner starts identifying what protocols they should use in trading, eventually they start to reap in some profits. The essence of these profits, though, is not to buy the latest trends and keep up with the most advanced technology. When managed properly, these profits can make even the most trivial of rookies into a dignified millionaire.

This skill set of money management is very useful in the fact that it entails managing risks and leverage. This allows the trader to last longer in the market without burning out.

The greatest danger lies in the leverage part.

There are a few things to consider in the whole process to achieve results:

Trade only the stocks that have a promising risk/reward ratio. This is where you compare what loses you'll incur as opposed to the profits on the stock. This ratio then should be at 3:1 with the profits being on the higher end to avoid an account blow up. This is one of the calculations you make while entering and exiting the FOREX market. Most traders assume this fact and end up regretting later. You should evaluate all the possible outcomes in a trade. You can never be having 100% guarantees that you will encounter a loss or a profit. Although, you can have predictions in which the ratio shows that there is a high likelihood of trade moving in a direction. Depending on the ratio, you can easily tell if an investment is worth taking or if you should avoid engaging in it at all costs.

These numbers aren't difficult to establish. There are certain pointers that will show you if you are wasting your time, or if it's a worthy investment. Such is essential in helping you make the right choices that can give you what you want. Instead of fully depending on luck to get your profits, it is good to get the facts right. The graphs and charts available in the FOREX market can help in coming up with some of these figures. You only need to keenly note how they move and come up with an appropriate ratio on how the trade is likely to move.

Set your trading platform to have a Max Dollar Stop-Loss. Sometimes, even seasoned traders are lured into making trades that eventually hurt the account due to eagerness. By having this limitation set, the rookie can avoid sudden moves on his account that might result in tragedy. This max dollar amount must help the trader sustain an 80% profit/loss margin. We tend to have huge expectations of increasing our earnings, and this can result in greed. You find that an investor keeps trading multiple times so that they can double their profits. This move results in overtrading, which is, at times challenging for you. To avoid this, ensure that you know when to exit a trade. This is a discipline that most people lack. You find that they keep engaging in trade without placing much thought and consideration into what they are doing. In the end, this issue bounces back to them, and they end up making huge losses.

A max dollar stop loss creates a limit for traders. It prevents them from engaging in more trades than they can handle in a day. This strategy helps them in minimizing potential losses and helps in boosting their earnings. At times you find that investors make losses in several trades, but they keep trading with the expectations that the next trade may earn a profit. That is more like gambling with luck, and the cards may work on your favor, or they may fail. If it happens that they keep losing in the other trades, the loss incurred will be huge, and they won't be able to recover from it.

While going for a loss, stick to a considerable limit. With day trading, as the exit hours near, people tend to get desperate and average down considerably. Use this chance to survive with your account by making your selling price a considerable amount to what you bought it for to avoid huge losses. This selling point also has the advantage to culminate into a profit-making venture. Making the right call is a huge challenge in options trading. Your daily decisions will determine the kind of trader that you will become. In life, we are faced with major challenges, and it is the decision that we make that allows us to win or lose our battles.

When you decide to go to a casino, you have high expectations that you'll win in the various games that you engage in. This thought crosses everyone's mind. You find that everyone hopes that they will emerge a winner. The sad truth is, there can never be two winners, one party has to lose as the other party walks home with a lot of cash. As you gamble, you must be open to the fact that you can either go home with a loss or a profit. Either way, it all depends on luck on that day and how tactical you were while playing.

This also applies to options trading. There are some tough decisions that you'll have to make; like being open to the fact that you can get a loss at any time.

Time your actions in order to make rational judgments on the stocks. This will allow you to calculate your moves without being rushed and thus avoiding losses. This is also significant when playing into a scene that will escalate into making profits. Each move that you make while trading options has to be well calculated. With the knowledge of the various options strategies, it gets easier to do this. You are probably wondering why I keep insisting on the options strategies. Well, they are the foundation of prosperous trades. You need to make sure that you're well aware of all the option strategies at your disposal if you intend to be an expert trader. These are the tricks that ensure if you walk away with a win or if you end up regretting the choices that you made.

For instance, we can evaluate the situation of players engaging in American football. It's a tough game, but a good strategy is what differentiates a loser from a winner. There are a lot of decisions to be made on the field. These decisions determine if a team will emerge a winner or a loser. The winning team usually has the right strategy and makes the right calls while playing the game.

This strategy also applies in day trading. A trader needs to know when to engage in a trade and when to avoid getting in a trade.

If the trade involves a higher risk, avoid it. At a point when one would be making losses, it is often observed that traders make hasty decisions and acquire more stocks in order to cover their losses. This is a tricky move as there is the risk of acquiring illiquid stocks or even run-down stocks which will burn the trader. The beginner needs to understand that losses are made in order to learn where not to go the next time, and that time should be given to improve the stocks. Observe the patterns so you can avoid these high-risk trades.

Part of trading involves analyzing the charts and graphs in the FOREX market. The information acquired from these graphs is essential in knowing how the market moves. It acts as a pointer in knowing the right way of doing things. Some of the trade moves that investors make are made with the intention of earning profits. At times, it turns out that they make the wrong call and end up regretting the actions that they made. The choices made by a trader count a lot while trading options.

These choices determine if they will earn a profit or make a tremendous loss.

Two wrongs can never make a right. We have had traders engage in a trade with the aim of compensating a previous loss. This may appear as a strong move to make, but it can result in a loss in the long run. You will be surprised that even after incurring another loss, some traders will still try making another trade which could end up in another loss. We have to make the right decisions while trading options and we should not expect too much within a short duration of time. Some efforts are required if we aim at being expert traders.

76

Chapter 11: Investor Psychology

The concept of investor psychology is a little vague and indeterminable. The very fact that 'psychology' is attached to it may deceive one into thinking it's something technical, something old professors grapple with. That is not so. Using illustrations, I will attempt to explain investor psychology using the simplest possible terms.

Simply put, investor psychology is concerned with the behavior of investors. It attempts to analyze how investors go about their investing process, how they think/react to situations, *etc.* This summation of the investing processes of investors then provides an insight into what works or not.

One of the chief reasons for investor psychology is to understand why some investors fail while others succeed. In the world today, there are certain investors who have become famous for their many strings of successes. That isn't to say that these individuals would not have experienced setbacks and failures. These individuals, however, have shown that continuous success is attainable.

Investor psychology studies these individuals and then tries to pinpoint why exactly they succeed. The result of this analysis is then used to create better investors. Also, it would help other investors avoid some of the mistakes they would have made if there wasn't a template to guide them.

You must realize that investing relies heavily on the psychology of the investor. Whether you would make profits or losses depends largely on your state of mind at every turn. Also, whether you would shake off the mistakes and forge ahead in the event of losses also depends on your strength of mind. While investing in acquiring knowledge, also invest in taking care of your mental health.

Psychological Traps That Work against Investors

Anchoring Trap

This is a situation where the investor relies only on former knowledge without letting in the room for new information. Investors sometimes make this mistake when they venture into investing. They work with the knowledge gathered from a myriad of sources – including the TV in some instances. This can be quite dangerous.

The truth is that you can never guarantee the credibility of the information you get from all these sources. The tips you have from long ago may have worked then, what is the guarantee that they still do today? There are companies that made the waves for their success story decades ago who aren't even relevant today.

At every point, you should be willing to re-evaluate your knowledge base to be sure what is currently working and what isn't. Endeavor to keep an open mind and to be receptive to new sources of information.

Confirmation Trap

This is usually the case with individuals who constantly seek advice from people who have made the same mistakes repeatedly. Ordinarily, there isn't anything wrong with making a few mistakes in your investing journey. Although, there are people who have failed repeatedly that it has become a pattern. You shouldn't be taking advice from this group of persons.

If someone gives you bad advice the first time, it might be instructive to check somewhere else next time. You would be saving yourself the trouble of making the same mistake repeatedly.

Relativity Trap

This is the unnecessary comparing of yourself with others and their experiences. This is particularly dangerous because everyone has a different psychological makeup.

Granted, there are some problems that affect everyone in the investment world. However, if it affects someone, it does not mean that it would affect you too.

Also, context is usually key in every situation. The opinion of others may not matter much outside of their own specific context. Invest only in the areas where you have the finances, interest, and experience for. Do not let anyone's opinion influence your investing pattern to your detriment.

Superiority Trap

Investors often fall into the trap of thinking that they know more than the experts in the field. They often make the mistake of thinking that because they have read a few books, they are good to go. That is a dangerous way of thinking.

The truth is, no matter how much you have read, or been told, nothing beats hands-on experience. The system is complex and can swallow you whole if you aren't properly guided. At the consent, you would need the help of individuals who have had experience in the field.

You may not necessarily need to employ the services of an account manager. This is especially so if you're just starting out and don't have a lot of funds. Although, there are certainly friends and family who have some experience in investing. You only need to ask them for help.

Develop a Clear, Concise and Workable Investment Strategy

To understand what an investment strategy is, you start with the definition of strategy itself. A sound understanding of the concept would help your understanding of what investment psychology is. Also, it would help in the development of a sound investment strategy.

A strategy refers to the process of developing a route to the attainment of a set objective. It talks about how a certain goal is to be achieved and the steps to be taken in its attainment. This implies that before a strategy is developed, there must be a goal set out to be achieved.

A strategy isn't as specific as an action plan. It views things from a broader perspective, answering the questions of how a goal begins and eventually completed. It is feasible to have more than one strategy in the pursuit of the attainment of a single goal. However, in its essence, all the strategies are supposed to eventually lead to the achievement of that one goal.

In developing his investment strategy, the investor focuses on investments that would yield steady returns over a longer period. An investor can go through this process with the advice of a consulting company. Sometimes, the investor could decide to embark on this process alone, choosing to employ the help of his immediate friends and family. This has its own benefit as well as its demerit.

The ability to develop and follow through with a strategy is a skill any investor can never do without. As we would discuss later, an investor without a strategy is like a rudderless boat. He moves at the behest of the wind, without any strategy charting the course for him.

Investing is a systemic endeavor. It involves articulate and methodical precision. When an investor lacks the foresight to develop an investment strategy, he hardly makes a profit from his investments.

The Importance of Having an Investment Strategy

There are several benefits to having an investment strategy. Especially a concise, workable strategy.

It Helps Minimize the Risk of Losses

For the entrepreneur/investor, the threat of losses always hangs over his head. At every turn, he is always assailed by the news of others who had invested the same way he did and incurred losses. It is for this reason that investors are always interested in any means to undercut losses and maximize their profit.

It Helps Provide Clarity on Your Long-Term Goals

For a lot of investors, investing is not a side hustle. They do not engage in investing in stocks, bonds, and securities for the immediate benefit. For many such individuals, they are in it for the long run. They usually will not be investing just for the immediate gratification they could derive from the investment. In that regard, having a strategy can prove to be helpful.

Opens You Up to the Possibility of New Opportunities For Your Business

Developing a strategy helps open you up to the idea of different other possibilities that could exist for your business. This is because, during this process, your creative juices get flowing. It does not mean that these opportunities would not have existed before that point. It also doesn't mean that they suddenly get created in that instant. What happens rather is that your eyes just get open to their possibilities.

It Helps in the Efficient Allocation of Time and Resources

Developing an investment strategy helps bring to your notice what has been working and what hasn't. You are made aware of the time and resources that aren't used effectively, giving you the opportunity to re-assign them. The result would be a more efficient investment process.

Criteria for Developing a Good Investment Strategy

It isn't just enough to have a strategy. In fact, having a terrible strategy is almost as bad as not having any strategy at all. The question then becomes: what strategy should an investor employ to ensure that his investment plan is top notch?

Make Sure Your Strategy Fits with the Overall Direction of the Investments

Before you decide on what strategy you would employ in the pursuit of your goal, you need to ask yourself some questions. First on the list is whether the strategy fits with the direction you have in mind concerning your investments. You should be sure why you want to invest. You should also be sure of how you want to invest.

Be Sure Your Strategy Matches the Resources You Have at the Moment

A good strategy proceeds alongside the estimate of the resources you have at your disposal. You should always choose a strategy that makes use of your resources have while maximizing returns.

Resources to be calculated include the finances you have, both in liquid and fixed assets. It also takes into consideration other intangible assets such as willingness and cooperation of friends and family. When all of these are taken into consideration, it will give an accurate depiction of your current state. Thus, it would then reveal the most feasible path to achieving your goals.

83

Chapter 12: How to Monitor and Grow Your Stocks

You can grow your stocks by rebalancing your portfolio when there's a need to do so. Remember the factors that you need to consider. There's also a need to monitor your stocks to make sure that you will consistently gain or only suffer minor losses. Understand that there are things that may suddenly affect the market trend but may not necessarily require you to sell your stocks right away.

You Need to Monitor the Business rather than the Price of Stock

There are times when the price of a stock keeps fluctuating. At first glance, it's quite alarming. As a wise investor, you need to monitor the business of the company where you bought some stocks. Understand also that sometimes some unknown situation may occur that can temporarily affect the stock price. Focus on the performance of the business and not the stock price. Provided the business is doing great, you can expect to get your future earnings from the company.

Analyze the Numbers

Your knowledge in technical analysis can also help you analyze the numbers or figures in the reports. You will know whether the sale is growing or not. If it's not growing, what is the reason behind it? Has the company increased its debt or issued more shares? There's always a reason behind each number.

Performance of Management

There are times when a change in management could affect the overall performance of the business. You need to know the management's sentiment towards the shareholders. Does the management pay dividends on time? What is the current focus of the management? You need to consider these and other related things to decide whether you will still get benefits and gains from your investment given the current performance of the management.

85

Chapter 13: Bonds and Government securities

Bonds are a form of debt, with the investor playing the role of a bank. Bonds are issued by a wide variety of entities, from municipal governments to corporations. The most famous bonds are those issued by the United States federal government. In this chapter, we will give an overview of bonds and how they work.

Bonds in detail

When you take out a loan, the bank gives you a sum of cash. You make payments on the loan, which will include paying some of the principal back with interest. A bond is a form of a loan, but instead of banks making the loan, investors loan the money. They don't work exactly like the type of loans you're used to; since the entity issuing the bond doesn't pay back the principal until the end of the life of the bond. And of course, if you want a car loan, you don't issue bonds to the bank.

Bonds are used to raise cash. A government may need cash for a wide variety of needs. Local governments can issue bonds to build roads, repair school buildings, or build new county hospitals. Typically, the bonds are voted on in local elections, and if voters approve the municipality will issue bonds to investors. Historically, municipal bonds have been a favored investment used by the wealthy, since they provide a tax shelter in addition to providing regular interest payments, hence generating income.

The federal government has used bonds, called U.S. Treasuries, to find budget shortfalls. As everyone knows by now, the U.S. government is in massive debt and yet continues to spend more money than it takes in – so it's continually issuing new bonds. Since their inception, bonds issued by the U.S. government have been extremely reliable, if not perfectly reliable. They are backed by "the full faith and credit of the United States." Even with the large debts the U.S. government has amassed, people worldwide remain confident in U.S. Treasuries and continue to invest in them.

The federal government also issues bonds to raise money for emergencies, in particular for wars. U.S. Savings bonds and liberty bonds are two well-known examples.

Corporations also issue bonds. They are often issued by top companies like Apple, Ford, and IBM. When you buy one of these bonds, you're lending the company money, so it isn't the same as a stock investment. If you invest in a bond issued by Apple, you have no ownership interest in the company. Apple will pay you interest payments on a regular basis, but when the bond is up (the 'maturity date'), Apple will return your principal.

Some bonds carry more risk than others. For example, there might be bonds issued by companies that have a bad history when it comes to paying the money back. These are called "junk bonds," and because of the higher risk associated with investing in junk bonds, higher interest rates must be paid. In recent times, some government entities are running into trouble meeting their obligations. On the opposite end of the spectrum from junk bonds that pay high yields or interest rates but carry a risk that you'll lose the principal (or that at some point they won't make the interest payment), are investment-grade bonds, issued by those with a solid record of paying their interest rates and returning the principal.

Bonds are considered relatively safe. In the stock market, in theory, you could lose everything. That isn't true with bonds since they are required to pay back your principal. For this reason, they are considered a safe investment. Although some governments are running into financial trouble, the taxation power of governments ensures that the investor has high confidence in the government paying back the principal on any bonds it issues.

Now let's familiarize ourselves with some jargon used when discussing bonds:

• Maturity: This is the end date of the bond. When the maturity date is reached, the principal must be paid back in full.

• Par Value: Also known as face value, this is the value of the bond when it's issued by the company or government. It is also the amount of principal you must invest in taking hold of the bond. The par value is noted because bonds often trade on markets after they are issued. Prices of bonds will rise, and fall based on prevailing interest rates. If the bond's price on the market is less than the par value, then it's a discount. If the bond's price on the market is higher than the par value, it's a premium. If you buy a bond directly from the issuing entity when it's issued, then you'll pay the par value.

• Coupon: This is the interest rate or yield on the bond. Yield is given as a percentage of par value. If you have a $1,000 bond with a 7% yield, then it will pay an interest payment of $70. Yields can be fixed rate, in which case the rate is constant over the lifetime of the bond, or they can be variable. Variable interest rates are pegged as a spread to some measures in the economy, such as the LIBOR rate which is a rate charged for interbank lending.

• Default Risk: The risk that the principal won't be paid back.

• Callable: A bond that can be called by the issuer at a date prior to the maturity date. Of course, if a bond is called, they have to pay back the principal. Since the issuer can call the bond at any time, the investor assumes more risk, and interest rates on callable bonds are higher.

• Puttable: If a bond is puttable, the buyer/investor can force the issuer to pay back the principal before the maturity date. Yields for puttable bonds are lower.

• Convertible: A type of corporate bond, which can be converted into common stock later. These bonds have a conversion rate, which is the number of shares the investor gets in exchange for converting the bond to stock. Convertible bonds pay lower interest rates. If the price of the shares, equal to the conversion rate, is greater than the par value of the bond, then it benefits the investors to convert the bond. If it's lower, then the investor would be doing a losing deal. When it's equal to the par value, then that is the breakeven price.

• Asset-Backed Securities: Bonds created that bundle together income streams from assets into a bond.

Bond Pricing

Bonds are bought and sold on secondary markets but not at their par value. Bond prices move inversely with interest rates. So, after a bond is issued, if the interest rate goes up, the older bond isn't worth as much. So, it will sell for a price below its par value, or at a discount. For example, if you buy a $10,000 bond with a coupon rate of 4%, which means you'll receive a $400 interest payment every year. Although, suppose interest rates go up and now the company issues bonds that have a 6% coupon rate. Now, someone can buy a new bond that will pay them $600 a year – so your bond is less desirable and so if you sell it on the market it has to be sold at a discount.

On the other hand, if interest rates drop, that makes the previously issued bond more valuable. Suppose that you buy a $10,000 bond that pays 5% interest, or $500 per year. Then, interest rates crater to 3%, so new $10,000 bonds that are being issued only pay $300 a year. That makes your bond a desirable investment, and investors will bid up the price and be willing to pay more than the par value to get a higher interest rate. In that case, you can sell more than the par value at a premium.

How to Invest

You can buy bonds from a brokerage. Some brokerages are municipal security dealers. You can buy treasuries directly from the federal government. Bonds can also be bought and sold on secondary markets, including through your own personal investment account that you self-manage. And as usual, you can invest in bonds through either a mutual fund or an ETF.

90

Conclusion

In the course of your trading experience, you must endeavor to learn from your adventures which is the most effective way to master a skill. Although a mentor or a teacher can help you, you will soon find out that the most influential opinion when trading is your own opinion so you must pay good attention to it and make it better. How can you make your opinion better? You can do this by possessing the right mentality when starting a trade. Whether the trade worked out or not, you must be ready to pick up yourself after losing a trade and focus again on the fact that you can make it again when trading next time. Having said that, you should also consider hiring a coach or get a mentor, someone who can always guide you in times when you experience difficulties in your trades. I hope you have been able to learn some simple yet effective strategies that will help you achieve success in your swing trading journey. Remember, always adhere to your strategy and be disciplined when trading.

I wish the best of luck in your trading.

92

CPSIA information can be obtained
at www.ICGtesting.com
Printed in the USA
LVHW080757010621
689024LV00011B/1003